The Goths

A Captivating Guide to the Visigoths and Ostrogoths Who Sacked Rome and Played an Essential Role in the Fall of the Western Roman Empire

© Copyright 2019

All Rights Reserved. No part of this book may be reproduced in any form without permission in writing from the author. Reviewers may quote brief passages in reviews.

Disclaimer: No part of this publication may be reproduced or transmitted in any form or by any means, mechanical or electronic, including photocopying or recording, or by any information storage and retrieval system, or transmitted by email without permission in writing from the publisher.

While all attempts have been made to verify the information provided in this publication, neither the author nor the publisher assumes any responsibility for errors, omissions or contrary interpretations of the subject matter herein.

This book is for entertainment purposes only. The views expressed are those of the author alone, and should not be taken as expert instruction or commands. The reader is responsible for his or her own actions.

Adherence to all applicable laws and regulations, including international, federal, state and local laws governing professional licensing, business practices, advertising and all other aspects of doing business in the US, Canada, UK or any other jurisdiction is the sole responsibility of the purchaser or reader.

Neither the author nor the publisher assumes any responsibility or liability whatsoever on the behalf of the purchaser or reader of these materials. Any perceived slight of any individual or organization is purely unintentional.

Free Bonus from Captivating History (Available for a Limited time)

Hi History Lovers!

Now you have a chance to join our exclusive history list so you can get your first history ebook for free as well as discounts and a potential to get more history books for free! Simply visit the link below to join.

Captivatinghistory.com/ebook

Also, make sure to follow us on Facebook, Twitter and Youtube by searching for Captivating History.

Contents

INTRODUCTION 1

CHAPTER 1 – WHO WERE THE GOTHS? NAMES, ORIGINS, AND EARLY SETTLEMENTS 4

    THE NAMES OF GOTHS 4

    ORIGINS OF THE GOTHS AND EARLY SETTLEMENTS 6

CHAPTER 2 – HISTORY OF THE GOTHS: RELATIONS WITH ROMANS, GOTHIC KINGDOMS 8

    GOTHS AND ROMANS 8

    GOTHS AND OTHER TRIBES 12

    GOTHIC KINGDOMS 14

        Ostrogoths 14

        Visigoths 17

CHAPTER 3 – OSTROGOTHIC AND VISIGOTHIC RULERS 21

    OSTROGOTHIC RULERS 22

        Ermanaric 22

        Valamir 22

        Theoderic the Great 24

        Amalasuintha 29

        Theodahad 31

        Ostrogothic Kings After the Amali 32

    VISIGOTHIC RULERS 35
        Alaric I *35*
        Athaulf *36*
        Theodoric I *37*
        Euric *38*
        Alaric II *40*
        Amalaric *41*
        Visigothic Kings After the Balthi *42*

CHAPTER 4 – THE CULTURE OF GOTHS: RELIGION, CUSTOMS, SOCIAL HIERARCHY 45
    RELIGION OF THE GOTHS 45
    CUSTOMS OF PAGAN GOTHS 46
    SOCIAL HIERARCHY OF THE GOTHS 48

CHAPTER 5 – EVERYDAY LIFE OF GOTHS: JOBS AND DIVISION OF LABOR, HOUSING AND ARCHITECTURE, ART, WRITTEN WORKS . 51
    JOBS IN GOTHIC LANDS 51
    HOUSING AND ARCHITECTURE 54
    GOTHIC ART 55
    WRITTEN GOTHIC WORKS 57

CONCLUSION – GOTHIC LEGACY IN EUROPE 59
BIBLIOGRAPHY AND REFERENCES 63
NOTES ON IMAGES 65

Introduction

When J. R. R. Tolkien was writing his best-known work, *The Lord of the Rings*, between 1937 and 1949, he drew inspiration from various sources, with the largest well of inspiration being European folklore. However, according to some sources, he would also use real-life historical figures and base his characters on them. Take Théoden, for example. Théoden was an aging king of Rohan who, after Gandalf the wizard helped him strip the yoke of Grima Wormtongue, rode into battle and died being crushed by his horse. The men picked him up and carried him into battle nonetheless, singing praises to him and shedding tears. Scholars claim that Tolkien based Théoden on a real-life king who also died by being trampled by his troops' horses but who was known for his bravery and who dealt a mighty defeat to a superior foe in the process. That king was Theodoric I, the battle was at the Catalaunian Plains, and the king himself was a Goth.

No, not the kind of Goth you might be imagining, dear reader. Centuries of Gothic subculture have left us with angsty teenagers wearing dark makeup, skin-tight leather outfits, and white face paint. But before that, the term "Gothic" referred to a particular type of literature, made popular by the 1764 novel *The Castle of Otranto* by Horace Walpole. It began a whole generation of prose and poetry that dealt with old architecture, churches, mysterious men and women, the supernatural, and the underlying element of fear. Yet even Gothic literature had to start from something. And since we've already mentioned architecture, it's instrumental to mention Gothic art and Gothic architecture. This particular movement was popular in pre-Renaissance Europe, taking some of the elements of Romantic architecture and art and putting a more "barbaric" spin on them. There are far too many churches, cathedrals, basilicas, and other buildings that were made in this style, but even that style had to derive its name from something. And if the terms "barbarian art" and "Gothic" are anything to go by, then the culprit is definitely the Goths.

Middle school level history will probably only mention the Goths in passing. You'll learn that they were divided into the Ostrogoths and the Visigoths at some point and that they were in the Roman service for a while. We won't blame you if that's the case. After all, for a long period of history, even proper historians avoided talking about the Goths. During the rise of the Nazi regime in Germany, Gothic and Arian ideas were freely interconnected with the totalitarian ideas of racial and national supremacy of Hitler's people. In fact, far too many people will think of swastikas and concentration camps if you so much as mention the term "Arian" to them. It's a huge shame that that's the case because those two terms are interconnected and make a huge part of European history. But we know better, dear reader. We will delve into the fascinating world of the Goths with a scientific lens, exploring everything we can about how they came about, where they lived, what they did, and how they died off. We will look into the nitty-gritty details of their everyday life, as well as some major historical events that were affected by Goths of any variety. Do strap yourselves in—there are quite a few of those.

Ancient and early medieval European history are replete with scant, contradicting, or even irrelevant information. Therefore, reconstructing an entire ethnic profile of a bygone people can be a daunting task. So, it shouldn't surprise you to spot some irregularities or unanswered questions in this book. But don't be afraid; even some of the greatest historians who studied the Goths, such as Herwig Wolfram, couldn't learn everything they needed to know (let alone everything they wanted to know) about the Goths. Hopefully, we will manage to rekindle some of that interest with this lovely volume you have before you. So, without further ado, let's delve into the world of the Goths.

Chapter 1 – Who Were the Goths? Names, Origins, and Early Settlements

One of the most common questions people ask historians is "Where do the Goths come from?" We know where they lived, what they did, and how they affected the course of human history, but we generally don't know anything concrete about their early days. Unlike the Sumerians, the Akkadians, the Babylonians, the Hebrews, and numerous other people groups, we can't exactly place the origin of the Goths, including how they got their name. Of course, there are plenty of different theories out there about the subject, but each and every one of them is debated fiercely by historians and archeologists even today.

The Names of Goths

The word "Goth" was, at certain points in history, a mere umbrella term for a wide swathe of different Germanic peoples. This isn't particularly odd since the Romans (and really any other people group in power) had the habit of not calling individual tribes by their actual name if they were replacing a tribe near the borders of their realm. For example, the Goths themselves were, at one point, called "Suevi," despite the fact that the Suevi was an entirely different people group. The same thing happened when they were called "Scythians."

In other words, when an ancient person would refer to the Goths, they would be talking about the Goths, Vandals, Rugians, Gepids, Scirii, Burgundians, and Alans, to name a few. But even the Goths themselves came in two distinct people groups (though why they came to be two groups is something we'll cover in later chapters). At the time, more specifically during the early and mid-4th century, they were known as the Greutungi and the Tervingi, but with the gradual rise of their prominence in Roman politics, they acquired different names. The Greutungi would bear the name Ostrogoths, later identified as the "Eastern Goths," whereas the Tervingi would gain the name Vesi, but even that was later changed (albeit by the Roman statesman Cassiodorus who had entered the service of the then-king of the Ostrogoths, Theoderic the Great) to Visigoths, the "Western Goths." Despite being essentially the same people, and even sharing rulers at a few points in history, the two tribes were very distinct, and the history of the Goths can't really be viewed in any other way than being the history of these two powerful and influential groups.

When it comes to the term "Goth" itself, the picture becomes a bit blurry. Historians have tried to link many "original names" to the tribe, such as Guti, Gutones, Gauts, Geti, and Getae. However, none of them have proven to be conclusively the same as the Goths of late antiquity, or even their ancestors. In Ostrogothic Italy, for instance, they called themselves the Gut-Thiuda, meaning "Gothic men," with many other variations existing in other languages such as Norse, Greek, and Latin.

One interesting theory is that the Goths got their name from a supposed major deity and the progenitor of the Gothic Amali royal dynasty, a god called Gaut or even Gapt. While not conclusive, it does offer good insight into how important the Amali actually were to the Goths if they were willing to name an entire people group after their first ruler.

Origins of the Goths and Early Settlements

The etymology of the term "Goth" does raise a lot of hot debates, but they are nowhere near as heated, diverse, or even controversial as the debates about where the Goths actually originated from. Many different places in Europe were suggested as their original homeland, but we can't claim with any level of certainty that they are accurate. One common example is the Scandinavian Gothic "original homeland." Despite a severe lack of physical evidence, many scholars still argue that the Goths came from the region that makes up modern-day Sweden. The 6th-century Eastern Roman historian Jordanes called this original Gothic homeland Gothiscandza.

If we did lend some credence to this theory, we can assume that the people group which would develop into the Goths came from Scandinavia to mainland Europe in the early 1st century CE. We actually have some evidence of an early Gothic settlement in modern-day Poland, as part of the so-called Wielbark culture. However, the site, which contains over 3,000 ancient tombs, didn't just "house" Goths. There's also evidence of Gepids, Rugians, and Venedi inhabiting the area, suggesting that all of these tribes (the Goths included) merely came here and settled an area where an earlier culture had lived. Whatever the case might be, the Goths (called Gutones by early historians) lived in the area and had to deal with other tribes on a daily basis. Three tribal groups in particular would wage wars and/or trade with the Gutones. The first were the Vandals, the second the Marcomanni, and the third were the Rugians and Lemovians (it's debated whether or not these two were the same tribe or if we should classify them separately). In later centuries, the Goths would begin to migrate eastward, inhabiting lands close to the Black Sea. This new culture was a melting pot of different influences. Other than the Goths, we also see traces of the Slavs, Dacians, and Sarmatians. Archeologists have dubbed it the Sântana de Mureș/Chernyakhov culture. The first part of the name comes from the commune in Romania where archeological localities of this culture are located. The second part is Soviet/Russian in origin, and it refers to the Black Sea.

It was here that the Romans first came into direct contact with the Goths, who called them the Scythians. We can safely say that they fully settled in this region in the first half of the 3rd century CE and that they were openly hostile to the Roman Empire. A Gothic ruler, Cniva, actually led a combined attack against the Romans with different tribes and possibly even Roman defectors among his units; it was an attack that would forever intertwine the fates of both the Romans and the Goths.

The region of Gotland in Sweden, with the island of Gotland in the east; some scholars still consider this region the original Gothic homeland.[i]

Chapter 2 – History of the Goths: Relations with Romans, Gothic Kingdoms

Goths and Romans

As mentioned in the previous chapter, Cniva was the first Gothic king (though the term "king" is debatable in this sense) to lead a successful attack on the Romans, winning the siege of the city of Philippopolis (today's Plovdiv in Bulgaria) in 250. But it would be the following year that really brought Cniva fame among the Goths and infamy among the Romans. During the Battle of Abritus (today's Razgrad in Bulgaria), Cniva crushed the Roman forces and killed both Emperor Decius and his co-emperor and son, Herennius Etruscus. The new emperor, Trebonianus Gallus, allowed Cniva to leave with all of his spoils and even agreed to pay him a tribute so that he wouldn't invade the empire in the future. This was a resounding success for the Goths, but more importantly, it was an evident sign that the Goths would become a prominent sociopolitical factor in southern and southeastern Europe.

Half a decade later, the Goths would begin to launch successful naval attacks against the Romans. It wouldn't be until Claudius

Gothicus, also known as Claudius II, became emperor of Rome in 268 that the battles between these two peoples would flip to Roman advantage. The emperor fought in several campaigns against a coalition of Germanic tribes known as the Alamanni, whom he defeated at the Battle of Lake Benacus. Immediately after this campaign, he turned his attention to the Goths, though they attacked first with the intention of invading Italy. It was in either late 268 or early 269 that Claudius' forces, led by his skilled commander Aurelian, crushed the Goths at the Battle of Naissus (modern-day Niš in Serbia). The death of Claudius in 270 brought about the issue of succession. By all accounts, Claudius' brother Quintillus was to take the throne, which he did with lots of support from the Senate. But the Roman army didn't accept him. Instead, they chose Aurelian as their emperor in Sirmium (Sremska Mitrovica, Serbia), and the two "emperors" clashed in battle. Aurelian took a decisive victory and became the legitimate emperor of Rome.

Aurelian's skill in combat was well known to the Romans. It was he who led the charge against the Alamanni while Claudius was still alive, and it was he who crushed the Goths at Naissus. But one more battle with the Goths would cement his name as a major military commander, and it took place in 271. Aurelian decimated the Gothic forces, killed their leader Cannabaudes, and forced them all beyond the Danube River. However, he relinquished all of the former territory of Dacia, a prominent Roman province in the Balkans and one of the first areas that the Goths inhabited en masse.

The Goths would fight Rome on several other occasions with varying success. In 275, they launched their last naval attack on Asia Minor, but the very next year, they were crushed by Emperor Marcus Claudius Tacitus. Half a century later, in 332, Emperor Constantine would systematically help the Sarmatians move to the northern banks of the Danube River. The Sarmatians were the first line of defense against the Goths, who were still raiding from time to time. According to local sources, the Goths lost over 100,000 people during these Sarmatian migrations. Constantine even captured a certain Ariaricus, who was supposedly the son of the reiks in charge of the Goths (we will get into the title of "reiks" and its relation to the term "king" a bit later). Even as early as this point, the Goths would have had a complicated relationship with the Romans. The vast majority of them acted independently and attacked the Roman borders frequently, but there were also scores of Goths who willingly fought for the enemy. Later history would prove to be just as complicated when it came to the issue of Goths being both allies and enemies of the Roman Empire.

The Goths didn't find any success in war until their rebellion which constituted the Gothic Wars of 376-382. During this time, the emperor who controlled the eastern part of the Roman Empire was Valens. During his reign, he had to put down a rebellion by Procopius, a Roman official who declared himself emperor in Constantinople. While Valens had to deal with Procopius, the Goths were preparing to rebel, which they did in tandem with a few other tribes in the Balkans (such as the Alans and Thracians). The barbarians and the Romans would clash in 378 at the Battle of Adrianople. During this battle, the Gothic chieftain Fritigern took a decisive victory and annihilated two-thirds of the Roman army. Valens himself was killed in a public burning. It was a humiliation that the Romans didn't expect, and many historians see this event as the prelude to the decline and fall of the Western Roman Empire (despite the battle taking place at Adrianople, which is in the Balkans which at the time was located in the eastern half of the empire).

But it didn't stop with Adrianople. The Goths were massacred in the streets in retaliation by Roman military officials, both soldiers and civilians. This prompted the Goths to rebel even harder, killing and looting everything Roman they could find. It was the task of the successor emperor, Theodosius I, to subdue the Goths, which he surprisingly did. At first, he would offer different Gothic tribes to either defect to Rome or be wiped out. His biggest diplomatic success that involved this tactic was when he negotiated with

Athanaric, one of the most prominent Visigothic chieftains and military tacticians at the time. While Athanaric himself died before he could definitively accept Theodosius' offer, his successors became ardent supporters of the Roman Empire. Theodosius even arranged for the late chieftain to get a huge, extravagant funeral, which awed the other Visigothic rulers at the time. In 382, the emperor turned his attention to the Ostrogoths, defeating their leaders in battle and sparing the survivors who surrendered. It was during this year that most of the Goths were allowed to settle south of the Danube border, with some moving into Asia Minor. Thanks to this maneuver, the Goths would become increasingly Romanized, while the Roman troops became more Germanic.

During this time, the Huns, a nomadic tribe from the east, were invading the Pannonian Basin and becoming a threat to the local tribes, the Goths included. The Goths were already undergoing a division, with the river Dniester serving as the de facto border between them. The Tervingi/Visigoths were loyal to the Roman Empire and became its foederati (semi-independent territories whose armies were tasked with defending Rome but who also received monetary and territorial benefits from the empire) whereas the Greutungi/Ostrogoths had to deal with the Huns.

Missorium of Theodosius I, Museum of Mérida, Spain. Note the Gothic soldiers left of the emperor, who is in the middle[ii]

Goths and Other Tribes

The Gothic people moved quite a bit throughout their several centuries of historical prominence. This allowed them to form relations with different tribes in their close vicinity, whether those tribes were under Roman rule or their direct enemies.

Probably the earliest tribe that we might ascribe as friendly to the Goths were the Taifals or the Taifali. This group would settle Dacia with the Goths, and as early as the 3rd century, they'd raid and attack the Romans under Gothic "kings." However, as time passed, the Taifals, like any other tribe close to the Roman borders, would enter into the service of the Roman Empire. After the fall of Rome, the Taifals were already under the service of Gaul. They more or less disappeared from history in the mid-to-late 6th century.

The relationship between the Taifals and the Goths was varied, to say the least. Since they were both Germanic in origin, they cooperated on many military outings against Rome. However, nothing really bound the Taifals to the Goths at the time, which is why they would fight against them whenever a significant number of Taifals entered Roman service.

When separate Gothic kingdoms formed, each of them had different tribes to deal with daily. The Ostrogoths, for instance, had a brutal and unrelenting enemy in the Huns. When it comes to the Balkans, historians argue that the Huns were a sort of "mortal enemy" to the Gothic people. The Goths would even use the Huns as parts of their curses and would accuse women of witchcraft and bearing children to the Huns. Fights between the invading nomads and the Goths in Dacia would be frequent and extremely bloody, which led to a kind of collapse of the Ostrogoths on a few occasions. Bizarrely, though, some Ostrogoths would outright join the Huns, either by means of surrender or by defecting from the tribe.

On the other hand, the Visigothic kingdom of Toulouse (which we will cover in more detail a little later) had other tribes that they were in touch with. Within the kingdom itself, several different people groups enjoyed civic freedom. Aside from the Goths and those Romans who willingly entered the services of their former barbarian foederati, the kingdom was composed of Syrians, Greeks, Bretons, and Basques, with a strong population of migrant barbarians such as Thracians, Galindians, Alans, Vandals, Taifals, some Gauls, Heruli, Varni, Thuringians, Saxons, Sarmatians, Suevi, and even Ostrogoths who fled from either the Romans or Huns. The Goths and the Romans, of course, held the highest power in the land, but they were very distinct, especially in terms of Christianity (Roman Christians vs. Gothic Arian Christians). Outside of the kingdom, the biggest threat to the Visigoths were the people of Gaul and, especially, the Franks. The Franks would be the ones to destroy the Visigothic kingdom, but before we move on to how the Gothic kingdoms fell, we should take a look at how they came about.

Gothic Kingdoms

Our history has known the Goths by two major names. They are either known as the Greutungi or the Tervingi or, thanks to Cassiodorus, the Ostrogoths and the Visigoths. Each of these kingdoms had a vibrant history that occurred alongside the fall of the Western Roman Empire and the rise of the West Germanic kingdoms in western and central Europe.

Before we move on to individual kingdoms, we should stress how we're going to approach both of them. Instead of going over every minute detail about each kingdom, we will treat you with a summary of how they came about. Each summary will start with their formative years and conclude with their fall. Finally, we will focus on the kings of the most venerated dynasties of both the Ostrogoths and the Visigoths in an individual chapter following this one.

Why the disclaimer? Well, the history of these two kingdoms is very messy and quite daunting, even for a seasoned historian. This way we can provide you with the most interesting details of the early Gothic kingdoms and how they shaped the political and social landscape of Mediterranean Europe, especially the Balkans, late antiquity Italy, and the Iberian Peninsula.

Ostrogoths

Ostrogoths are indeed interesting on the face of it, especially if we look at their lineage. Many different rulers claimed divine origins throughout Europe, and the rulers of the Eastern Goths were no exception. As we said, the Goths didn't really have a hereditary system of rule, but that didn't stop them from having their dynasties, and the mightiest house to rule the Eastern Goths were the Amali.

Historically speaking, it's hard to trace some of the older rulers of this dynasty. It would be interesting if we could since one of the ancestors, right under Amal (the so-called Father of the Amali), was called Ostrogotha. Of course, the name itself could have been a contemporary construction during the time when Cassiodorus wrote his major work, the *Origo Gothica*, or the history of the Gothic people. Be that as it may, we can't say for certain if the first ten or so rulers of the Amali dynasty even existed as actual, non-mythical figures. The first Ostrogothic ruler for whom we have some kind of confirmation of historicity is Ermanaric. According to Roman sources, most notably the *Res Gestae* (Latin for "Things Done") by ancient historian Ammianus Marcellinus and *Getica*, a work by the Roman historian Jordanes which claims to be the summary of *Origo Gothica*, Ermanaric ruled a wide portion of land known as Oium. Supposedly, this land was a section of Scythia which the Goths had recently moved into during the time of Ermanaric's direct ancestors. Experts disagree on just how much territory this reiks had under his belt, but they're fairly sure that he was a prominent political force in the region.

Ermanaric ruled the Gothic lands (according to some historians, they stretched from the Baltic Sea to the Black Sea) until his death. He was then succeeded by his brother Vithimiris, who more than likely ruled around the year 375 or 376, according to Marcellinus. Jordanes, on the other hand, claims that the ruler who took over after Ermanaric was a different king, Vinitharius.

If we take Marcellinus at his word, Vithimiris would die in 376 fighting against the Huns, so his kingdom was ruled by two chieftains, Alatheus and Saphrax, who served as regents for Vithimiris' infant son, Videric. Both of these men would prove themselves as capable soldiers, and Alatheus would distinguish himself at the Battle of Adrianople in 378, where they were allies with the Tervingi chieftains Fritigern and Alavivus. We don't know for sure what happened to Saphrax, but Alatheus would continue to lead military campaigns against the Roman Empire, eventually dying in battle in 386 when his army tried to invade the Roman territories south of the Danube.

If we take Jordanes at his word, however, we find a few more rulers such as the aforementioned Vinitahrius (the so-called Conqueror of the Venedi-Slavs) and his son Vandalarius (the Conqueror of the

Vandals). Each of these rulers supposedly led the Goths during the reign of Attila the Hun (434-453), though there are other sources mentioning other rulers such as a certain Videric (or Vettericus), son of Berimund and grandson of Thorismund. Thorismund was supposedly the son of Hunimund the Younger, who in turn was the son of Ermanaric. This section of the Amali family tree is indeed convoluted, and this is only one branch. Ermanaric's supposed descendants would eventually take hold of the Ostrogothic lands through marriage, which we will cover a little later. For now, let's focus on Vandalarius. According to the early sources, he had three "sons": Valamir, Theudimir, and Vidimir. In truth, these three chieftains were merely brothers-in-law. Valamir succeeded the previous reiks, starting off as a loyal vassal to Attila the Hun and completely taking control of the Gothic lands many years after Attila's death. His reign ended either in 468 or 469. Both Vidimir and Theudimir ruled after him, with the latter's reign ending in 474. Theudimir's son and heir Theoderic (or Theodoric) would be one of the greatest rulers in Ostrogothic history (and Gothic history in general).

The Ostrogothic kingdom had its roots in the Balkans. However, at its peak between 493 and 553, it encompassed the whole of Italy and Dalmatia, covering parts of today's Italy, Austria, Slovenia, Croatia, Bosnia and Herzegovina, and Switzerland. Moreover, Theoderic was the king of both the Ostrogoths and the Visigoths at one point, cementing the reign of the Amali dynasty over all Goths. After his death, the kingdom would wane and fall due to dynastic disputes. It would see its end when Byzantine Emperor Justinian I began his conquest of the former Western Roman territories. Archeologists and historians aren't in full agreement over the year, but it's generally thought that 553 was the year when the Battle of Mons Lactarius took place. During this battle, the last of the Ostrogothic kings died, and the Eastern Goths lost their independence for good.

Visigoths

While the Eastern Goths fought against the Huns, the Western Goths were forced to flee. In the year 376, a large contingent of Goths left Dacia to evade attacks from the Huns and settled south of the Danube, accepting Roman rule. However, their relations with the Romans quickly soured, which led to massive rebellions and wars. The year 378 and the Battle of Adrianople would prove to be a defining year for all the Gothic tribes, with a decisive victory against Rome and the murder of Emperor Valens, but it was four years later that the seeds of division between the two Gothic tribes would be sown. Emperor Theodosius I officially settled the ancestors of the Visigoths in the province of Moesia, making them the foederati of the empire. Their task was to safeguard the northern border against the invading tribes. In exchange for their service, the Goths were given lands and titles. Bit by bit, these once pagan tribes began to convert to a new form of monotheism, known as Arian Christianity. A little over a decade later, in 395, they would follow Alaric into the territory of today's Greece. By 401, Alaric had already begun to raid Italy, with large numbers of his Goths beginning to settle the peninsula. Alaric has the honor to be known as the first Visigothic ruler whom we can historically verify and is commonly referred to as the founder of the Balthi dynasty, the royal house of the Visigoths.

Alaric would also be the first ruler in late antiquity to completely sack Rome in 410. Because of his exploits, he became a major threat to the empire, and his death (which happened the same year) only barely felt like a relief. Half a decade later, his successor, Athaulf, would take the Western Goths even farther west, settling them in Gaul (modern-day France) and the territories of modern-day Spain.

The Visigoths had a tumultuous history during this period. Their own relations to Rome were dodgy and shifted often. However, the monarchs that followed Athaulf cemented Gothic power on the Iberian Peninsula, as well as its supremacy over the waning Roman

Empire. Athaulf was succeeded by a chieftain called Valia, who in turn was succeeded by Athaulf's nephew, Theodoric I. It would be Theodoric who would be the first chieftain history recognizes as a king rather than a mere reiks. This monarch's history is filled with military successes and expansions, and his life ended in the most glorious way possible—he was the king who defeated Attila the Hun at the Battle of the Catalaunian Plains and made him retreat, a battle where the Gothic king lost his life in the thick of the fray.

Theodoric's sons would prove to be just as famed as their father, but an infamous tradition of fratricide marked the Balthi at the time. Theodoric's eldest son Thorismund, for example, succeeded him in 451, but as early as 453, he was usurped by his younger brother Theodoric II and killed. Theodoric ruled for thirteen years, having both lost and reclaimed the region of Septimania (today's French Riviera that encompasses the French Mediterranean coast) in wars against the Romans. During his defeat, the Visigoths retreated as far west as the region of Aquitania (southwestern France). This particular move by the Goths would prove to be important because of what Euric, the younger brother of Theodoric II, was going to do. Namely, Euric killed his brother in 466 and assumed the Visigothic throne, ruling for eighteen long years of prosperity. During his time, the Visigoths invaded and conquered most of the Iberian Peninsula, with the city of Toulouse as their capital. In 475, Euric would officially declare himself an independent ruler, severing ties with the Roman Empire.

Euric's reign was plentiful. He codified the first Gothic laws, whose fragments survive to this day. In addition, he was a staunch Arian Christian, and the Church flourished under his dominion. He would be succeeded by his son Alaric II, who himself codified his own code of law. An ally of Ostrogothic King Theoderic the Great, he married his daughter Theudegotha and had a son with her called Amalaric, who would rule the Visigoths from 526 to 531. But Alaric also had an illegitimate son, Gesalec, who was elected by the people to rule after Alaric's death in 507 in the Battle of Vouillé against the Frankish king Clovis.

Alaric's death was the de facto end of the Balthi-led Visigothic power. They still maintained control of Septimania, however, with Narbonne as their capital. But they never reclaimed the vast territories that both Euric and Alaric II controlled. As the centuries passed, the Visigoths living in the remnants of Euric's kingdom converted from Arianism to Catholicism. The kingdom would begin its rapid decline after the Battle of Guadalete in 711, where the Gothic Christians lost to the Muslim Umayyad Caliphate led by the commander Ṭāriq ibn Ziyad. Some kings held out until 721 and the conquest of Narbonne; after that, the entire Iberian Peninsula submitted to Muslim rule.

At its height, the Visigothic kingdom (also known as the Kingdom of Toulouse or the Kingdom of Toledo) stretched from the south of Spain to the southwest of France, excluding some territories that belonged to what is now modern-day Portugal and parts of northern Spain. It was a true European powerhouse at the time, and its influence still echoes in the region. The kingdom also established the Visigoths as a political and religious force, with its rulers surviving the fall of the Western Roman Empire and the rise of other barbarian kingdoms in the Mediterranean.

Relief detail of the Ludovisi Battle sarcophagus, National Museum of Rome. The scene depicts Romans and Goths in battle[iii]

Chapter 3 – Ostrogothic and Visigothic Rulers

The term "king" doesn't really apply to a Gothic ruler. While we will go into more detail about this when we cover the social hierarchy of the Goths, we will only briefly mention that the title "reiks" isn't necessarily the same as the title of king. Of course, many rulers who styled themselves as reiks were also historically Gothic kings. So, to make things a bit easier, we will use the title of "king" interchangeably with that of "reiks" for all of the rulers below.

Both the Amali and the Balthi dynasties produced statesmen of incredible skill and fervor. It's actually rather stunning that a tribe whose origins are modest at best was able to achieve such prominence that they would be able to outshine even a powerhouse like the Roman Empire. Some of these kings were also direct participants or direct witnesses to some of the most famous historical events of early Europe. As such, they are definitely worth a detailed, thorough read.

Ostrogothic Rulers

Ermanaric

Although not the progenitor of the Amali dynasty, Ermanaric is certainly a ruler that left his mark on the ancient world. Supposedly, he was in charge of a massive territory that took up a large section of today's Ukraine. If we are to believe the ancient sources, that territory would stretch from the Danube River in the Balkans to the Baltic Sea in the north, as well as between the rivers Dniester and Don.

According to Marcellinus, Ermanaric took his own life when the Huns began to invade and plunder his kingdom. Other sources mention conspiracies to poison the Gothic ruler and other potential ways that could have ended his life, but the veracity of these claims holds little historical weight.

There is more legend than fact written down and passed on when it comes to Ermanaric. He supposedly conquered many different tribes like the Finns, the Slavs, and the Estonians, as well as securing an alliance with the Western Goths (though it's far more likely that he forced them to submit as well) and driving the Vandals out of Dacia. Because of his many military achievements, he became a legendary king in many different European cultures. The Anglo-Saxons and the Scandinavians especially grew fond of the famed Amali ruler, and he was shown as being a powerful but ruthless king. Whatever the case might be, Ermanaric is the first historically known Amali monarch among the Goths, but he would definitely not be the last.

Valamir

Valamir, according to tradition, ruled the Ostrogoths after a 40-year-long interregnum, i.e., a period without a ruler. He is supposedly the first ruler to hold dominion over a large portion of the Goths in the

Balkans after his cousin Thorismund, the grandson of Ermanaric. However, historically speaking (and if we take all of the sources into consideration), it's highly likely that the rulers who came before Valamir were vassals to the Huns, who were now a major force in Pannonia and at their peak under the reign of Attila. Valamir's father was a ruler called Vandalarius, while his brothers-in-law (and his short-lived successors) were Theudimir and Vidimir.

Valamir became a powerful warrior while he was in Attila's vassalage. In 447, he would raid the lands below the Danube alongside the Huns and distinguish himself as a strong ally. In the Battle of the Catalaunian Plains, he was one of many commanders that led Attila's army. It seemed as if Valamir would continue his loyal service to the Huns, but Attila's death in 453 changed all of that. Shortly after this event, Valamir began to openly solidify his position as ruler after Emperor Marcian settled the Goths in Pannonia. Valamir rebelled against Attila's sons and continually defeated them in a series of battles. Between the years 456 and 457, he would finally crush them and win independence for the Goths.

But Valamir was having both external and internal problems when it came to his rule as an independent monarch. Namely, an Amali collaborator of the Eastern Romans appeared in the form of one Theodoric Strabo. Strabo is a Roman term for people who were crossed-eyed, which would translate his name to "Theodoric The Squinter." Strabo was on good terms with the Romans and their emperor, Leo I, and he would receive large tributes as a reward for his service. Valamir's Goths, on the other hand, didn't receive their share in 459. This prompted a series of attacks on the province known as Illyricum, and these attacks would not end until three years later. Emperor Leo agreed to pay Valamir's men 300 pounds of gold on a yearly basis to maintain good graces with the Goths.

In 469, there was tension brewing between the Ostrogoths and a lot of minor Germanic tribes. This coalition of tribes was led by the Suevi chieftain Hunimund, the Scirii chieftains Onoulf and Edeko, and a certain Alaric, and the tribes in question were the Suevi, the

Scirii, the Sarmatians, the Rugians, the Gepids, and possibly the Heruli. Of course, the Roman Empire officially supported the anti-Gothic coalition, hoping to crush the Goths and gain a huge swath of territory. Theodemir, the brother-in-law of Valamir, was the chief commander of the Goths. The two sides would clash in the Battle of Bolia, and while we might not know the exact number of casualties, the historical consequences of this war tell us enough. Namely, the Goths crushed the coalition of tribes and practically ended the Scirii for good. However, there was one important casualty during this war: the reiks himself. Valamir was thrown off his horse during a raid by the Scirii a little before the battle. He was subsequently killed, allowing Theudimir to take control of the land.

Theoderic the Great

Coin depicting Theoderic the Great, Palazzo Massimo, Rome[iv]

There is little debate when it comes to the question of the most famed Gothic ruler in all of history. Proper Ostrogothic history might even be said to begin with the son of Theudimir, with a man who would come to raise the Goths from a disjointed barbarian tribe to a major political force in all of Europe.

Theoderic was, almost prophetically, born in 454, the very year after Attila's death. At the age of seven, he was sent to Constantinople as a hostage to Emperor Leo I; this was done so that the emperor could ensure that the boy's father, the aforementioned Theodimir, would honor his part of the treaty. However, this situation proved to be beneficial to the young Goth. He would gain an education from the best teachers the Great Palace of Constantinople had to offer. As such, he learned and spoke both Greek and Latin, though we can't say with what fluency he did so. Emperor Leo admired the young man, as did his successor, Emperor Zeno.

After 471, Theoderic was no longer a hostage to the Romans. Eight years later, he would settle the Goths in Epirus with the help of his cousin and a skilled warrior, Sidimund. It's worth noting that Sidimund was in the service of Valamir, Theoderic's uncle-in-law, making him a commander with noteworthy battle experience.

The year 483 saw the young Theoderic become the Roman "Master of Soldiers." The next year, he was elected as a consul during a lavish ceremony which Emperor Zeno presided over. But Theoderic would eventually return to his people in 485, and sure enough, three years later, he became the king of the Ostrogoths.

Theoderic would claim his first major historical footnote during the early days of his reign over the Eastern Goths. It had been twelve years since the Western Roman Empire fell to Odoacer and his troops. The Germanic king's ruthless reign left former Roman citizens in Italy essentially without any human rights. In addition, he would often go after the Byzantine lands near the borders of his new kingdom. Zeno, wanting to calm the now restless Goths and to rid himself of Odoacer, proposed that Theoderic invade Italy, an endeavor which he gladly accepted.

At first, Theoderic won a few minor battles, such as the ones in Isonzo and Verona in 489. The Battle of Faenza was his first major defeat against the Italian king, but he quickly got back on his feet at the Battle of the Adda River in 490. For the next three years, Theoderic would lay siege to Ravenna, which was the capital of Odoacer's Italy at the time. Both monarchs agreed to a peace treaty which was to be marked by a banquet on March 15, 493. During this banquet, Theoderic performed a deed that got him into the history books. He proposed a toast to Odoacer but then jumped at the defeated king and struck his collarbone with his sword. With this action, Theoderic became the man who defeated the destroyer of the Western Roman Empire. Italy now belonged to the Amali.

Theoderic's reign in Italy was a breath of fresh air to the residents. The Romans retained their rights, and the Gothic king maintained good relations with the Byzantine emperor. The Romans lived under their own law and customs while the Goths, now the ruling class, lived under theirs. Even other minor religious groups were allowed to practice their faith. In the year 519, an angry mob burned Ravenna's synagogues. However, Theoderic ordered the people of the city to pay for the complete rebuilding and restoration of these sacred Jewish places.

Theoderic saw the importance of allies early on, so he began to form relations with different tribal kings by way of marriage. He himself married Audefleda, the sister of the Frankish ruler Clovis I. His own sister Amalafrida was married off to an incompetent Vandal king called Thrasamund, with whom she had two children that we know of. However, the marriages of Theoderic's daughters were far more intriguing and important to the Goths. Theudigotho, his oldest daughter, married the Visigothic king Alaric II, with whom she had one son, Amalaric. With that move, Theoderic was essentially ruling over the Visigoths by proxy, since he was the regent of his infant son after Alaric was killed in a battle in 507. His second daughter,

Ostrogotho, married Sigismund, the king of the Burgundians at the time. Sigismund would eventually order his men to kill their son Sigeric in 522, shutting down the Amali dynasty's potential claim to the Burgundian throne. Sigismund's second wife, according to the medieval Gallo-Roman historian Gregory of Tours, supposedly asked him to deal with Sigeric because he was plotting against the Burgundian throne and that he even had ambitions to inherit Theodoric's throne in Italy.

And the marriage of his youngest daughter, Amalasuintha, proved to be the least fruitful in terms of establishing a long-term dynasty. Amalasuintha married an Ostrogothic noble who lived in Iberia at the time. This man was named Eutharic, and, based on tradition at least, he was the distant relative of Ermanaric, which technically made him an Amali noble and the right person to inherit Theoderic's throne. However, Eutharic died in either 522 or 523 while Theoderic was still very much alive.

While his kingdom was in disarray at this point, Theoderic wasn't one to give up. When his grandson Sigeric was killed, the king of the Ostrogoths invaded the Burgundian lands and in 523 annexed the southern parts of the barbarian kingdom. Sigismund himself was a prisoner, and his brother, Godamar, ruled what was left of the Burgundian territory. With this campaign, Theoderic's kingdom was at its territorial peak. Sadly, the following year would see the Vandal king Hilderic capturing Theoderic's sister Amalafrida and killing her Gothic guards. From that point until the end of his life in 526, Theoderic was planning an expedition to free her.

Theoderic was known for his military prowess, his acute sense of politics, and for his just attitude toward the many different ethnic groups that lived within the borders of his kingdom. However, he was also a renowned builder as well as a renovator of old Roman architectural sites. Ravenna saw the majority of his rebuilding efforts, where he reconstructed an old aqueduct which provided fresh water for the city. Ravenna was also the home of his now-famous Palace of Theoderic, which contained a small church and an equestrian statue of the king. In addition, he issued the building of Hagia Anastasis, an Arian cathedral, as well as three other churches. Ravenna also holds his mausoleum, a rare architectural feat of its time.

Rome was also a city that the king loved to reconstruct and "repopulate" with new buildings. He rebuilt the city walls, the granary, the sewage system, the aqueducts, the Senate's Curia, and the Theater of Pompeii. The Senate itself gifted Theoderic with a golden statue of himself as gratitude for his work on the walls. Possibly his biggest undertaking in the city was the reconstruction of the Palace of Domitian on Palatine Hill. His endeavors in these fields were so well known that even people in Syria were singing praises of the Gothic king.

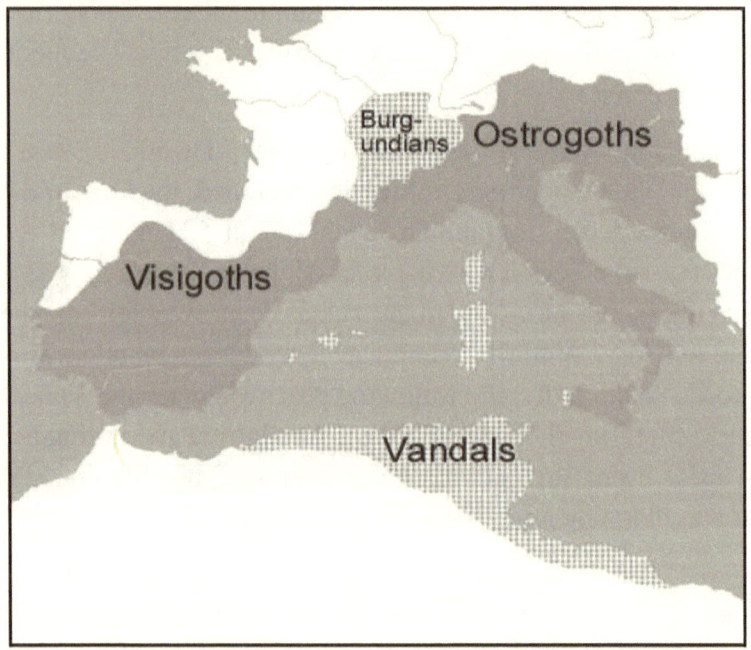

Theoderic's kingdom at its peak, c. 523. The solid pink territory is directly ruled by Theoderic, whereas the gradient territories represent his vassals[v]

Amalasuintha

Amalasuintha is an odd addition to this list, but she was incredibly influential to the events that would follow the death of her father and the dissolution of Ostrogothic Italy. During Theoderic's reign, she was married to Eutharic, an Amali noble from the branch of Ermanaric. This was done specifically because Theoderic wanted an heir with a pure Gothic royal bloodline, making Eutharic the perfect choice. However, Eutharic himself died during Theoderic's reign, so he was unable to succeed the great Ostrogothic monarch.

With both her husband and her father gone, Amalasuintha was effectively the ruler of the Ostrogoths in 526 since her son, Athalaric, was only a ten-year-old child at the time. The Gothic queen also had a daughter, Matasuntha, who would go on to marry one of the later Gothic kings roughly a year after her mother's death.

Athalaric was a king in name only. Over 90% of the political decisions were coming from Amalasuintha, and nearly every decree or legal document was done through her engagement and nearly none of his. While Amalasuintha's reign was largely peaceful at first, the Gothic nobles didn't take too kindly to her, mainly because she held deeply rooted Roman values and virtues and sought to pass them onto the young heir. The nobles wanted to educate the young king in their own values, which caused a rift between the queen and the nobility. Athalaric himself was drawn to drinking and other excesses which made him physically weak and incompetent. He would die on October 2, 534, at the age of eighteen. Amalasuintha would remain the queen for another year, co-ruling Italy with her cousin Theodahad.

The Gothic queen was a model woman during her time. She was fluent in Greek, Roman, and Gothic, and she also had extensive knowledge in philosophy and politics. With her affinities to everything Roman, it is no wonder that she was in frequent diplomatic contact with Byzantine Emperor Justinian I, known as the greatest ruler that the court of Constantinople ever had. Justinian and Amalasuintha maintained good relations throughout her reign, and she even wanted to move to Constantinople with a vast part of the Gothic treasury.

But not all of Amalasuintha's decisions were wise. Her co-ruling with Theodahad, for instance, was a move that looked good on the surface. As the firstborn of Amalafrida and the son-in-law of Theoderic the Great, Theodahad was respected by the Gothic nobility, so his co-regency of Ravenna with his cousin would turn Amalasuintha's detractors into allies. However, Theodahad more than likely sided with the Gothic nobles because Amalasuintha was imprisoned in 535 and taken to the island of Maltana, a landmass in Lake Bolsena. She was murdered there the same year, leaving Theodahad as the sole ruler of Ravenna. Historians aren't in agreement about Theodahad's involvement with the killing of Amalasuintha; some say he was responsible, while others claim he can only be involved to the extent of ordering her imprisonment.

Her death was the event that initiated the Gothic War, which lasted until 554 when Italy was crushed by the Byzantines. Justinian's ambitions to return Rome to its former glory were slowly coming into fruition, and the catalyst for all of it was the death of the Gothic queen at the hands of her own people.

Woodcut of Amalasuintha, The Nuremberg Chronicle, 1493[vi]

Theodahad

Theodahad ruled in Ravenna for a very short period, between 534 and 536. He was an elderly man at the time of his ascension and preferred poetry and Neoplatonic philosophy over matters of war. While he was far from being the first ruler to have this disposition, he was ruling the kingdom during its notable downfall. The Byzantines were not happy with the death of Amalasuintha, an event which Theodahad might have had nothing to do with. Nevertheless, Justinian's troops, led by his famed general Belisarius, began invading Italy promptly, and it was the general's successful invasion of Naples that sealed the Gothic king's fate, considering he hadn't sent any help to the natives of this city. With the civil unrest and the threat of Justinian quite literally at their door, the Goths wanted Theodahad out. One Ostrogothic noble, Vitiges, was declared the new king of Ravenna. His marriage to Amalasuintha's daughter Matasuntha cemented his claim to the throne. His very first act after the marriage was to depose and kill Theodahad, to the joy of the local Gothic nobility and people alike.

It's a little sad to see just how inconsequential Theodahad's reign had been. If we look at the rulers that followed, we come to a startling realization that Theodahad was the last Amali king to rule over the Ostrogothic people. A powerful dynasty that crushed numerous tribes and kingdoms and rose to hold a vast area of southwestern Europe in its fist ended with an elderly monarch who ruled for no more than two years.

Ostrogothic Kings After the Amali

With Theodahad deposed and killed, the reign over what was left of Italy went to Vitiges, the first non-Amali ruler to sit on Ravenna's throne. He would merely be the first of five kings to reign over a failing kingdom during Justinian's conquest, collectively known as the Gothic War, which lasted from 535 to 554.

During its early stages, Vitiges was already married to Matasuntha, giving himself at least a tenuous link to the Amali dynasty. He immediately had a massive problem on his hands, though, that being the siege of Rome by the Byzantines. The two armies would clash for control of the city from 537 to 538, an endeavor which ended with Justinian's victory and Vitiges' retreat. A huge chunk of the Byzantine army was made up of Huns and Slavs, two tribes that had historically clashed with the Goths frequently while the Roman Empire was, at least nominally, still a single realm. But it wasn't just manpower that defeated Vitiges. Justinian's troops were better trained than their Ostrogothic opponents, and Belisarius was an experienced military commander who had already won a host of different battles.

Losing Rome, Vitiges would begin his retreat to Arminium (modern-day Rimini, Italy), but Belisarius took this city as well—not through battle, but rather through intimidation. When his army was joined by 2,000 Heruli bannermen led by an Armenian eunuch called Narses, the Byzantine general divided his troops into three separate garrisons, all of which began to surround the city. Vitiges had no other option but to flee. The same year would see the fall of towns such as Aemillia and Urbinum.

The first victories for the Goths came between 538 and 539 when the Byzantines unsuccessfully tried to take Mediolanum (modern Milano). This endeavor saw the removal of Narses from the position of commander and gave Belisarius complete control over the armies. Another somewhat interesting defeat came to both the Byzantines and the Goths when a huge host of Franks descended from the Alps and attacked the two armies. They were victorious, but an outbreak of dysentery halved their ranks and forced them to retreat. This event gave both armies some time to recuperate and draw up new battle plans.

Ravenna was the final destination for the Byzantines and the last place of refuge for Vitiges. During the war, he tried to find allies in different rulers, even going so far as to contact the Persians and ask them to attack the eastern frontier of Byzantium. Sadly, all his efforts, thus far, had failed, and Vitiges was all but deposed. Justinian's court offered lenient terms with the empire keeping parts of Italy south of the river Po and the rest remaining under the Goths. While both the Ostrogothic nobility and the Byzantine generals accepted these terms, Belisarius did not. However, when he was in Ravenna, he was offered the title of Western emperor, which he falsely accepted. Vitiges was made a patrician, but that didn't stop Belisarius from taking both him and Matasuntha as hostages to Constantinople in late 540. Vitiges died childless in 542, while Matasuntha married a Byzantine patrician called Germanus, who was a cousin of Emperor Justinian. The two had a single son, also called Germanus, who was born in 551.

The vacant spot of the king of the Ostrogoths had to be filled. A lot of Gothic nobles wanted to see Uraias, who was stationed in the town of Ticinum (modern Pavia), succeed Vitiges. This made sense as Uraias was both the greatest military commander in the Ostrogothic army and the nephew of the previous king. But Uraias refused the throne in favor of Ildibad, who controlled Verona. Ildibad himself was a Visigoth, a nephew of the first non-Balthi Visigothic king Theudis. They both controlled the only specks of free Gothic land, but Ildibad, upon ascending the throne, quickly expanded his reach to Venetia and Liguria. One of his best-known victories in battle was that of Treviso, where he crushed the local Roman military commander Vitalius. Of course, Ildibad wasn't alone. Aiding him in his efforts were the Heruli, whose leader was killed in combat. Ildibad's authority over the valley of the Po River grew with each victory, and his own nephew, Totila, became the military commander of Treviso.

The very next year, 541, saw Ildibad murdering Uraias under the suspicion that his uncle's clan was plotting to remove him from power. Later that year, Ildibad himself was murdered at a banquet. Since there was no suitable heir, Eraric was elected as the successor to the now-late Visigothic noble. Eraric was a Rugian, and his tribe was one of the many allies that the post-Amali Ostrogoths had. However, he was far from being the best choice of monarch to succeed Ildibad. Namely, he had secretly been planning to surrender the kingdom to the Byzantines, a plot which was thwarted by the Goths. Totila, the nephew of the late Ildibad, vied for power in Ravenna and demanded the death of Eraric, a demand which he saw come true that very same year. With Totila at the helm, the Ostrogoths would see ten years of relative stability and revival.

Totila's skills as a commander were shown early on when he began to push back the Byzantine army. Soon after, he would take control of the southern Italian Peninsula, getting ready for bigger and harder sieges. One such siege was of the city of Naples in 543, which ended with the city opening its gates to the king due to starvation. Totila would go on to lead no less than three different sieges of Rome. The first one in 546 was successful; it was also helped by tactical starvation of the inhabitants, but the city remained steadfast and quickly rebuilt its walls. During the second siege, Totila was defeated by Belisarius, but the success was short-lived as the Byzantine general was recalled from Rome. During the third siege in 549/550, the city opened its gates to Totila, this time thanks to a few starving Romans who defected to the Ostrogothic king.

Moving onto Sicily, Totila conquered Sardinia and Corsica, after which he shifted his attention to Greece. Under Justinian's orders, General Narses advanced against the Goths, and the two armies clashed during the Battle of Taginae in 552. Totila was killed in combat, and his death was the final nail in the coffin of the Ostrogothic kingdom.

The last known king of the Ostrogoths was Totila's distant relative and army commander Teia. Teia ruled for only about half a year, and his rule was marked with difficult battles, retreats, and skirmishes. His capital was Pavia, but he would meet his end close to modern-day Naples during the now-famous Battle of Mons Lactarius. General Narses crushed the Gothic forces, and Teia himself was killed in combat, just like his predecessor. Most of the Gothic generals were killed in combat as well, and those that survived sought an armistice. A mere year later, in 554, all of the Gothic lands were subjugated, and the people began to assimilate with the local Italians.

Visigothic Rulers

Alaric I

Though merely a reiks, Alaric I had proven himself to be a capable ruler well before the Kingdom of Toulouse was established. Possibly his greatest achievement was the sack of Rome in 410. It was the first time a foreign invader had captured the city in over 800 years. However, the sack itself wasn't as devastating as many other sieges that came before or after it. The Gothic armies merely burned a few buildings and plundered them for riches. The Roman citizens themselves were spared any inhumane acts. In addition, the basilicas of St. Peter and Paul were nominated as sacred places not to be disturbed (other than plundering).

Sadly, Alaric would meet his end the very same year he sacked Rome. While he was in Calabria in the south of Italy, Alaric wanted to invade Africa. However, most of his ships were battered during a storm while he sailed south with his troops. The reiks himself died in Cosenza, more than likely from a fever.

Alaric's name became legendary, so much so that a few rulers were either named after him or had a name that was some variation of his.

Athaulf

Athaulf was a brother-in-law to Alaric and succeeded him as reiks immediately after his death. Athaulf's reign was mired in controversy, political intrigue, and complicated relations of Roman emperors and pretenders to the throne. However, he was the first Visigothic ruler to secure territorial autonomy and political prestige to the Gothic tribes.

Athaulf and the contemporary emperor of Rome, named Honorius, had a complicated relationship. At first, Athaulf would frequently support pretenders to Honorius' throne, such as Priscus Attalus, a man whom Alaric had made emperor in Rome to rival Honorius' rule in Ravenna. In addition, the Visigothic ruler had an important hostage, the emperor's half-sister Galla Placidia, which might have secured him gold and territorial autonomy from Ravenna. During his trip to Gaul, where he would have joined forces with the local usurper Jovinus, Athaulf came across Honorius' Gothic commander Sarus. This was a significant encounter since Sarus and Alaric had had a long-standing rivalry, which Athaulf deepened by murdering Sarus. Once again, Honorius had an additional reason to go to war against the Visigothic leader. But then things took an unexpected turn. Jovinus declared his own brother Sebastianus as co-emperor, an action which Athaulf didn't approve of nor knew about. Enraged, Athaulf allied himself with the emperor in Ravenna and crushed the two usurpers, slaying Sebastianus in battle and capturing Jovinus in Valentia in 413.

The very next year, Athaulf took Galla Placidia's hand in marriage. This move cemented the relationship between the Western Roman Empire and Athaulf's Visigothic people. Placidia gave birth to their son, Theodosius, but the child died in infancy a mere year later.

During 415, the final year of his life, Athaulf had already been ruling over Narbonne and Toulouse, which he took in 413. His relations with the Roman Empire soured thanks to Honorius' general, Constantinus, a man who would later be crowned Emperor Constantinus III. Athaulf and Galla Placidia were traveling west, and while in Barcelona, the Visigothic reiks decided to take one of Sarus' men into his service. The same man killed him in his bath, which prompted the ascension of Sarus' brother, Sigeric, to the position of king. But Sigeric would "rule" for a grand total of seven days, promptly getting killed and being replaced by a non-Balthi ruler, Valia. During his reign, Galla Placidia returned to Ravenna in 417 and married Constantinus III, the same general who had a major falling out with the Visigoths.

Theodoric I

Valia ruled for only three years, after which he was succeeded by Theodoric I. Although he was an illegitimate son of Alaric, he was nonetheless elected as a monarch of the Visigothic people. It's interesting to note that an illegitimate son would go on to become one of the most glorious rulers of his time. The famous Battle of the Catalaunian Plains, where his efforts helped crush Attila the Hun and marked the end of Hunnic supremacy over the Balkans, was merely one of his many accomplishments. During his reign, he expanded his kingdom to the Mediterranean coast, taking Narbonne and Toulouse. He also made allies with both the Vandals and the Suevi by means of marriage; two of his daughters married Huneric of the Vandals and Rechiar of the Suevi. However, Huneric would later have different ambitions which excluded the Visigoths, so he had his wife mutilated and sent to Theodoric. From that point forward, Theodoric saw the Vandals as enemies.

Theodoric's valor against Attila was and still is historic. However, it goes beyond dying in battle. Namely, in order to fight the Huns, Theodoric and his sons made an alliance with a famed Roman general named Flavius Aëtius. Aëtius and Theodoric had been bitter rivals during the entirety of his reign, but the ruler of Toulouse recognized the danger Attila posed to contemporary Europe, so he set aside his differences with the Roman commander and marched against the Huns. This determination and prudence in the face of battle cemented Theodoric as one of the most beloved historical figures of late antiquity.

Euric

Statue of Euric at the Plaza de Oriente, Madrid, Spain [vii]

Theodoric I was succeeded by his son Thorismund, who in turn was succeeded by Theodoric II, and who himself was succeeded by possibly the greatest Visigothic monarch and the first proper king of the Western Goths, Euric. These ascensions to the throne, however, were rather grim. Namely, the oldest son, Thorismund, was killed by Theodoric II in 453, an act which Euric himself continued by killing his older brother in 466. He would go on to rule the unified Visigothic kingdom for eighteen long years.

Euric's ambitions began roughly at the same time the Western Roman Empire was about to collapse. At the time of his reign, Toulouse was the capital of the Visigoths, but the Visigoths themselves were still disunited, with some factions following different chieftains. One by one, he would defeat them and take their land as his own. But his true military prowess showed when he had to deal with wars outside of his realm. During the Battle of Déols in 469, he defeated Riothamus, the king of the Britons, and claimed a huge portion of his territory which might have gone as far as the river Somme. Two years later, in 471, Euric would win a major battle in Arles where he killed, among several Roman officials, Emperor Anthemius' son, Anthemiolus. It was also during this year that Euric issued the first ever Germanic code of law, the so-called *Codex Euricianus*.

He was rather popular with his people, and even a significant portion of the Iberian and Gallic Romans also saw him as a fit ruler. Ambitious as ever, Euric demanded in 475 that the current Roman emperor, Julius Nepos, recognize Visigothic territorial sovereignty and Euric as its independent ruler. While each Visigothic reiks that came before Euric was only nominally a Roman vassal, the vassalage was still valid. Euric made history in 475 by becoming the first independent Visigothic king and starting his own dynasty, that of the Balthi. In that same year, as well as in 476, he laid siege to the city of Clermont-Ferrand.

Until his death in 484, Euric had ruled nearly all of the Iberian Peninsula, as well as a third of what is now modern-day France.

Aside from being a skilled fighter, he was also an incredibly learned man with a wealth of knowledge and wisdom. It's no wonder that many of the Romans living in Iberia willingly acknowledged his kingship and why even priests saw him as a model king.

Visigothic kingdom at its peak under Euric, c. 500. Everything in orange is Visigothic, with the light orange being the territory lost after the death of Alaric II[viii]

Alaric II

In contrast to his father, Alaric II is seen historically as an incompetent, weak ruler when compared to Euric. However, he did have his own fair share of political and military successes. For instance, he famously assisted Theoderic the Great in his campaign against Odoacer in Italy, helping him during his brief capture in

Pavia in 490. Possibly his biggest contribution to the Visigoths in terms of battle was the capture of the city of Detrosa in 506.

When it comes to contributions in the legal sense, Alaric II appointed a commission that would draft an abstract which contained Roman imperial laws and decrees. Roman subjects living under Alaric were to follow these sets of laws. They are commonly known as the Breviary of Alaric, or *Breviarum Alaricianum*.

Alaric's death would come in 507 at the infamous Battle of Vouillé. Years before the battle, Alaric had a rival with the Frankish king Clovis and was, in fact, intimidated by him. The two had already produced a treaty in 502, and Clovis was on good terms with Theoderic the Great, but it didn't stop him from moving his troops into Visigothic lands. Alaric met Clovis on the battlefield and, as contemporary sources claim, lost his life to the Frankish king himself.

Alaric's kingdom lost a good portion of its lands after his death, most of them to the invading Franks. However, the worst blow to the kingdom was the incompetence of his heirs and the dissolution of the Balthi rule over the Kingdom of Toulouse.

Amalaric

Amalaric was the legitimate son of Alaric II and Theoderic's daughter, Theudigotho, making him both Balthi and Amali by blood. However, he was not the first son of the Visigothic king. The first son was the illegitimate Gesalec, who was voted into succeeding the throne because Amalaric was just an infant at the time. However, Gesalec was an incompetent ruler who was overthrown in 511 when his capital, Narbonne, was plundered by the Burgundian king Gundobad. Theoderic took control of the kingdom, acting as a regent for his grandson until he came of age. Gesalec would be killed sometime in 513.

Amalaric would eventually grow up and take the Visigothic throne in 522. During his reign, he married Clovis' daughter Chrotilda, but according to some contemporary sources, he wanted her to convert to Arian Christianity and had even beaten her to the point of bleeding. Her brother was Childebert I, the king of the Franks, and after he was sent a towel stained in her blood, he took action against Amalaric. Childebert's army crushed Narbonne, and the Visigothic king was forced to flee to Barcelona in 531. During his time there, he was assassinated by his own men, with some historians suspecting that Theudis, the king that would succeed Amalaric, was somehow involved.

Amalaric's death as the last of the Balthi is a bit of a sad footnote in history. For most of his life, he was no more than a puppet for his grandfather's ambitions. Even his name clearly tells us who the dynasty in charge was during the waning days of the Visigothic kingdom. While the Amali would continue to rule for a while longer in Ostrogothic Italy, the Balthi would more or less cease to be with the death of this king.

Visigothic Kings After the Balthi

Visigothic Spain remained largely independent throughout the 6th and 7th centuries until it was crushed by Muslim Umayyad invaders in 711.

The list of kings that followed the Balthi dynasty holds an amazing number of 25 kings. During their reign, the old Kingdom of Toulouse would hold different names, such as the Arian Kingdom of Hispania and the Catholic Kingdom of Toledo. The kings in question include Theudis, Theudigisel, Agila I, Athanagild, Liuva I, Liuvigild, Reccared I, Liuva II, Witteric, Gundemar, Sisebut, Reccared II, Suintila, Sisenand, Chintila, Tulga, Chindasuinth, Recceswinth, Wamba, Erwig, Egica, Wittiza, Roderic, Achila II, and Ardo.

Of these kings, the monarchs of historical note are Theudis, Reccared I, Suintila, Recceswinth, and the last three kings on the list. Theudis was the first non-Balthi monarch of the Visigoths and got his claim to fame as a sword-bearer of Theoderic the Great. Theudis was a skilled warrior, but he was also a monarch who respected the Church and even showed leniency toward Catholics, which wasn't very common of Gothic kings that practiced Arian Christianity. His descendants would rule the Ostrogothic kingdom in its waning years after he was killed in his palace by a man who pretended to be mad in 548. Saint Isidore of Seville, an archbishop and a scholar at the time, wrote that Theudis, as he lay bleeding on the floor, ordered for his murderer to be spared because the murder was just Theudis paying his dues for a similar crime, i.e., the murder of his monarch.

Reccared I ruled from 586 to 601. His ascension to power would result in the most drastic change in Visigothic religious history. The very next year, in 587, Reccared would renounce Arian Christianity and declare himself Catholic, and most of his closest allies in the Church followed suit. This move, however, led to many Arian uprisings, all of which the king squashed. Reccared also showed a massive intolerance toward the Jewish population, prosecuting them and formally forbidding their religious practices. He would die of natural causes in his capital, Toledo.

Suintila's reign was marked both by peace and by the reclaiming of territories which the Byzantine Empire held under its control. But more importantly, it was Suintila who saw the importance of unifying the Iberian Peninsula, using the term "mater Spania" for the first time. Linguistically speaking, this was the first time in history that the term "Spain" was used in these lands.

Recceswinth ruled from 649 to 672, and interestingly, outside of a single rebellion, Spania enjoyed a period of peace from 653 up to the death of Recceswinth. Much like Reccared I, Recceswinth was anti-Jewish, but he was tolerant in other aspects of his political career. In 654, for example, he sought to replace the Breviary of Alaric with a new code of laws that the Hispano-Roman citizens were to follow. This was the enhanced and enriched version of the Liber Judiocorum which his father, Chindasuinth, promulgated back in 642 or 643. It was notably more influenced by Roman laws with very little Germanic influence. While he was in power, the church councils became the highest authority in the kingdom, almost rivaling that of the monarch.

In terms of the last three kings, we should note a historical discrepancy. Roderic was often cited as the last Visigothic king before the Umayyad Caliphate invaded Spain in 711. While it is true that the king was defeated by the Muslim commander Ṭāriq ibn Ziyad at the Battle of Guadalete, Achila II was also in power during this time, probably as a rival to Roderic. We know very little about either of the two rulers, but we can ascertain that Achilla held only a small portion of the old Visigothic kingdom when the Umayyad invaders began their conquest. Ardo is the very last king of the Visigoths whose historical records we actually have. He ruled between 714 and 721 for a grand total of seven years, more than likely defending a small section of territory (Septimania and modern-day Catalonia) from the Muslim invaders. With his death and the capture of Narbonne, the last vestiges of the Visigothic kingdom were gone.

Chapter 4 – The Culture of Goths: Religion, Customs, Social Hierarchy

Religion of the Goths

Not much is known about early Gothic paganism. We can reasonably surmise that it was a form of an old Germanic polytheistic religion and that they had a similar pantheon to early Scandinavian Germans. However, it should be noted that the Goths took great pride in their ancestors and that they deified them. The Amali dynasty is the perfect example of this, considering they saw themselves as the successors of Gapt or Gaut. Many of Gapt's aspects are similar to Odin/Wodan, further giving credence to the hypothesis that the Gothic pagan religion was largely Germanic in composition. Two other possible Gothic gods that we have some evidence of are a god of war—possibly an equivalent to the Germanic Tiwaz—and a god of thunder known, presumably, as Fairguneis.

While we barely know anything about the Gothic pantheon of gods or mythical creatures, we do know quite a bit about their pre-Christian customs. Each Gothic village, called a kuni, had a sacrificial meal as a tribute to an idol of a pagan god. A Gothic reiks would oversee the ceremony, but he would have other important roles as well. Namely, if a Goth were to reject the ceremony or the pagan faith as a whole, it was the role of the reiks to protect the tradition and punish the non-believers. Oddly enough, even in the early days of the 2nd century when they were migrating to Roman Scythia, the pagan Goths didn't particularly mind the local Roman Christians and usually left them to their own devices. However, they were brutal to Gothic converts to Christianity.

A few sources speak of Gothic witches or "haliurun(n)ae," women who apparently practiced sorcery and gave birth to Huns. Tribal leaders dealt with women suspected of this practice by exiling them. In addition, the Goths began to engage actively in practices of their immediate neighbors, such as the Taifali. For example, they would practice pederasty, as well as the early pagan rite of passage. A boy had to slay a four-legged wild animal in order to rid himself of "uncleanness" and become a man. And speaking of clean and unclean, the Goths also took sacred oaths and believed in demonic possession. But it wasn't just dark magic that the Goths believed in. Light magic and miracle-working were also a major part of their everyday religious repertoire.

Customs of Pagan Goths

It's extremely difficult to talk about the earliest customs of ancient Goths since there are barely any written accounts on their culture and everyday life to begin with. However, we do have some idea of their customs during the time they were inhabiting the Roman Empire. When we read the texts describing the passion of St. Sabbas the Goth, mainly letters from contemporary priests, we learn quite a bit about the daily lives of Gothic people inside of a village. This includes the religious practices that Sabbas, a Christian, refused to partake in. For example, we learn that the Goths had a possible tradition of parading a wooden idol in a cart through the village which people had to bow and pray to. From linguistic sources, we can also speculate that the early Goths practiced ritual sacrifice since the terms for both sacrifice and sacrificer are used in a different context in the Gothic Bible. An important part of these rituals was eating the sacrificial meat. Tasting meat from a non-sacrificed animal or even refusing to eat meat altogether resulted in a horrific punishment. In the case of St. Sabbas, it was exile.

Another important custom of the Goths comes to us from their graves. Most Germanic tombs store a variety of different objects that the people buried with the deceased for various religious or political reasons. A non-Christian Anglo-Saxon nobleman, for example, would be buried with jewelry, weapons, and food to show off his level of social prestige. Later Christian graves would eliminate this practice as it was seen as extravagant and not compatible with the humble, ascetic nature of Christianity. However, there's an interesting discrepancy with Gothic pagan graves. Based on the finds in the tombs that belong to the Sântana de Mureș/Chernyakhov culture, archeologists discovered that every Gothic grave which involved inhumation (i.e., burying the body in the ground as opposed to burning it first) didn't contain any weapons. Apparently, early Gothic pagans never buried their dead with weaponry, which is quite different from the vast majority of other Germanic tribes in Europe. Some scholars note that the practice of burying swords and armor wasn't even common with the Germans of ancient Europe until the 5th and 6th century when the Goths were already Christianized.

Visigothic necropolis, Sisopo, Spain[ix]

Social Hierarchy of the Goths

As stated earlier, the term "king" doesn't really work with distinguished Gothic rulers, or at least not until King Theodoric I (some would argue that his son Euric is actually the first to have an actual title of king, however). The title each Gothic ruler had was "reiks," which sounds a lot like the Latin *rex*, and *rex* does translate as "king." But a Gothic reiks wasn't a king in the traditional sense. There was no law or tradition where a child of the Gothic ruler would become the next reiks. He had to be chosen by the tribal council, which, if we take the Gothic Bible as a relevant linguistic source, was probably called "gafaurds." The council was made up of the "maistans" and "sinistans," the magnates and the elders, and next to the reiks, they were the most privileged people in the Gothic community. And while we're on the subject, the Gothic community had a very interesting name, "kuni," with the plural being "kunja." This term is interesting because it has linguistic relations to terms like kin and even king.

So, what was the role of a reiks? In terms of the oldest known Gothic tribes, he was the local chieftain and a supreme judge. But as the Goths became more and more independent, he would take on a number of roles. We will take a look at the Visigothic kings of Toulouse as an example. Within Arian Christianity, for example, the reiks was the head priest, which was more than likely a carryover from Gothic pagan tradition. Next, he was the commander-in-chief of the Gothic army and would always be in the front lines of battle. Moreover, he was also the highest legal authority in the Gothic state, establishing laws and passing sentences if and when needed. And finally, he conducted all affairs that had to do with foreign policy. However, he didn't have complete power. The council of magnates and elders was still very much in effect during the time of the Balthi dynasty.

Each kuni had its own shrine, its own priests, and more than likely its own specific cult. They also had their own small armies; an army was called a "harjis" in Gothic, and it numbered roughly 3,000 men. One subdivision of a harjis was called a "hansa," but we can't ascertain how large a single hansa might have been.

Most of the upper classes lived in large estates. The reiks, for example, lived in a "baúrgs," a fort (this is also a term that possibly relates to the word "burgh" which means "city, dwelling"), while the nobles (the "fraujas") lived in a large fortified house called a "gards." Interestingly, while the baúrgs only housed the reiks and his family, the gards would be the home to not just the family of a noble but to all of his servants. His estate would house slaves ("skalks"), day laborers ("asneis"), the "magus" (a title of unclear origin), and other types of servants. Different reikses would have different nobles and servants pledge their loyalty to them, which led to the formation of clans ("subja"). Despite the Goths slowly becoming more stratified vertically (with kings, priests, and nobles at the top and slaves at the bottom), the horizontal stratification in the form of clans was still an important part of their society.

Most of the Gothic people were freemen, i.e., not slaves but not members of the nobility. They would live in a village, a "haims," away from the reiks and the nobles. We know quite a bit about the Gothic village from the story about St. Sabbas, which was written down and spoken of by some of his contemporaries. Namely, the village had its own assembly which handled all the local decisions. However, they couldn't affect the council of nobles and, more importantly, the nobles could very well nix any decision the village assembly made.

Chapter 5 – Everyday Life of Goths: Jobs and Division of Labor, Housing and Architecture, Art, Written Works

Jobs in Gothic Lands

Several early sources paint a picture of the Goths as being predominantly forest folk with very barbarian, nomadic lifestyles. However, one invaluable document gives us a clearer insight into what this ancient people actually did in their everyday life. One 4th-century Gothic bishop of Greek descent, Wulfila, underwent a massive task of translating the Bible from Greek to Gothic. For this task, he crafted an entirely new alphabet using Germanic runes and the Greek alphabet as a basis. Of course, some sources claim that the translation was more than likely an effort of a whole team under Wulfila's supervision.

We pay close attention to the so-called Gothic Bible because Wulfila described everyday events using contemporary terms. In other words, he used Gothic terminology to describe different jobs and occupations in biblical stories, terminology that was without a doubt used by the Goths. Of course, these words come to us from the

Visigothic lands, which means that the Ostrogoths and other tribes associated with the Goths might not have used the same terms, though we can't be certain about this.

From Wulfila's translation, we can ascertain that the Goths were avid farmers. They plowed many types of fields, called "akrs" and "thaurp" with plows called "hoha." They would use oxen, or "auhsa," to pull the plows, and they would link them with a yoke, called a "jukuzi." Some of these words, like "auhsa" and "jukuzi," clearly correspond with the modern English equivalents of ox and yoke as both Gothic and English are Germanic languages in origin. The Visigoths sowed many different types of grain, or "kaurn." Their fields contained wheat ("hwaiteis"), rye ("kaurno"), barley ("barizein"), as well as flax, or "saian," which they used to make linen ("lein"). The group word for these green crops was "atisk." A typical farmer would use a "giltha," a sickle, during a harvest ("asans"), which usually took place in the summer. Carts, or "gajut," took the reaped wheat for threshing to a place called a threshing yard, "gathrask." After the threshing was done, the grain would be stored in "bansts," barns. Once there, the Gothic farmer would grind the grain using a circular hand mill, a "quairnus." It was then up to the baker to bake raised dough ("daigs") and make flatbread, "hlaifs." However, based on contemporary sources, the Visigoths didn't yield a lot of grain from these agricultural practices. That's why they had to rely on importing Roman grain, at least during the time of Emperor Valens in 366. Aside from agriculture, the Goths had some minor skills in gardening, but no source from that time tells us just how efficient they were.

Animal husbandry was also more than likely practiced during the early Gothic times. Based on food remnants and scarce animal bones in Gothic graveyards, we can safely state that the Goths raised cows, sheep, poultry, horses, and donkeys. They would use the latter two for transportation and as beasts of burden. Sheep, in particular, were useful for their wool, which the Goths used for clothing. Cows yielded milk, while chickens laid eggs; both of these were essential foods for the Goths, next to meat.

Aside from farmers and animal husbandmen, there was a whole slew of different professions in ancient Gothic lands. Some of them include:

- blacksmiths ("smitha" or "aizasmitha")

- carpenters ("timrja")

- butchers ("skilja")

- clothiers and fullers ("wullareis")

- fishermen ("nuta" or "fiskja")

- healers or early doctors ("lekeis")

- potters ("kasja")

Each of these trades was important for the everyday life of a Goth. A blacksmith would work on weapons and iron tools. Interestingly, they also made a massive number of combs and fibulae (brooches for fastening clothes). Carpenters would make wooden furniture using small hand-axes. Both butchers and fishermen provided a Gothic village with food in their own separate ways. Fullers and clothiers worked on wool to make clothing. And naturally, a healer was always necessary for the weak and the sick.

Potters, in particular, are important for historians and archeologists because it's thanks to them that we have a whole host of Gothic artifacts that survive to this day. They would fashion different pots of various sizes, but they also made oil lamps that were similar to their Roman counterparts. Pots were mass-produced and more than likely exported to other lands in the region.

Trade was a major part of Gothic life, and the Romans were by far the biggest trading partner if and when that was possible. The Romans would export wine and cooking oil to the Goths, as well as fine fabrics and jewelry. All of these items were highly valued by

Gothic nobles and wealthy houses at the time. For example, Gothic men of wealth would drink wine in heavily adorned cups and goblets, and the women would wear elaborate jewelry made of silver and precious gems. Whenever a war would break out between the Romans and the Goths, trade would cease, and the Goths would suffer heavy shortages. It's no wonder that they would always claim free trade during the times of peace. While they did have raw materials and material goods to trade, the Goths would often use slaves as payment. Whenever there was a surplus of people (Gothic or non-Gothic), the Goths would go to Danubian slave markets and sell them off to the Romans.

Housing and Architecture

Going over the Sântana de Mureş/Chernyakhov sites, we can spot fascinating finds that tell us about the houses of early Goths. Two different types of homes existed based on how they were built. The first reminds us very much of early Anglo-Saxon dwellings, where the houses were built with floors cut into the ground. These sunken huts are what archeologists call pit-houses, or "Grubenhäuser" in German (the singular form is "Grubenhaus"). The pit-houses of the Goths were either rectangular or oval, sometimes even half-oval. Normally they would be very small, covering anywhere between 5 and 16 square meters, or 54 to 172 square feet. The floors were just beaten earth, whereas the walls were made of daub and wattle and the roofs were made of rushes. Some of the dwellings of the Goths near the Black Sea even had stone floors. Each and every house had a hearth for heating during the winter months.

The second type of house that the Goths would inhabit is the surface house. In German, these homes are called "Wohnstallhauser," or byre-dwellings. The name itself perfectly explains their purpose—they contained two parts under one roof: the living quarters of the family and the animal section. They also came in two different sizes. Small byre-dwellings would measure 10 to 30 square meters (107 to 323 square feet), whereas large ones would go up to anywhere between 68 and 128 square meters (732 and 1,337 square feet). Both types of houses had plastered walls and timber framing, rushes as roofing material, beaten earth floors, and stone hearths.

These differences in size and material are not there for nothing. Wealthier Gothic families could afford bigger, sturdier houses for themselves and their extended family. This was especially true with the Gothic nobles who were either on good terms with the Romans or who enjoyed a lot of wealth in the village for one reason or another.

Gothic Art

It's unfortunate that the term "Gothic art," as well as "Gothic architecture," is related to a movement that happened centuries after the last of the Gothic kingdoms was long gone. We have barely any proper examples of how Gothic artists might have expressed themselves. However, there must have been some noteworthy level of skill. For example, if we look at the basic brooches, belt buckles, combs, personal jewelry, and the pottery of the Sântana de Mureș/Chernyakhov culture, we can see that the effort put into some of these pieces was not just to be useful but also aesthetically pleasing. Possibly the most famous example of this is the Visigothic eagle-shaped fibula made of gold, bronze, meerschaum, glass, and gemstones in the 6th century. The eagle motif was a carryover from the Roman tradition, and people in the Balkans would continue to use it well into the Middle Ages.

One particular style of fashioning jewelry that ancient Goths perfected was the polychrome style. They would use wrought cells and encrust gemstones into whatever gold object they were making. This method continued into the Middle Ages in southwestern Germanic Europe well after the Gothic kingdoms were already formed.

Top: Visigothic eagle fibula, 6th century; Bottom: Ostrogothic crossbow fibula, 5th century [x][xi]

Written Gothic Works

Like Gothic art, we know next to nothing about their written works, largely because ancient Goths didn't have a unified writing system. However, there are a few artifacts that scholars assume contain Gothic runic inscriptions. Three of them are seen as authentic Gothic writing before Christianization, one of which is a ring from Pietroassa, Romania, and two of which are spearheads found in Ukraine and Germany.

But with Christianity, the Goths did get a much-needed addition to their culture—the Gothic alphabet. During the 4th century, Wulfila created a system of 27 letters that corresponded to sounds in the Gothic language. His translation of the Bible was, by all means, a step in the right direction for the Christianization of the Goths, but more importantly, it opened the door for learned, intelligent, and literate monarchs. Aside from this translation, we don't have any other written work that uses the Gothic alphabet, translated or original. Moreover, we don't even have the complete manuscript of the Gothic Bible. Instead, we have fragments that survived as five separate codices and a lead tablet containing some Gospel verses.

Spearhead of Kovel, Ukraine, with Gothic runic inscriptions probably noting the name of the weapon[xii]

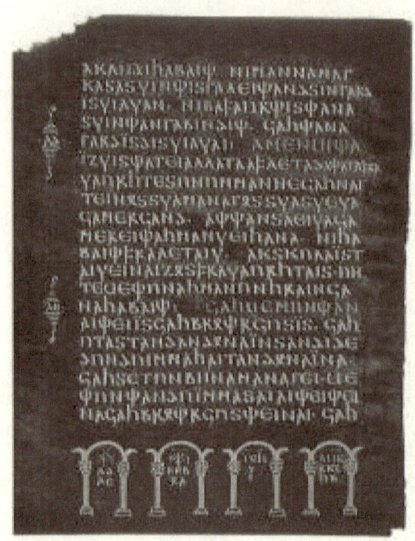

A single page from Codex Argenteus, the longest manuscript that contains Wulfila's Gothic translation of the Bible[xiii]

Conclusion – Gothic Legacy in Europe

The Goths, overall, did more to change the political and cultural landscape of Europe than most people between the 4th and 8th centuries. It's no wonder that two massive movements in art and architecture use the term "Gothic" in their name.

The Goths were incredibly adaptable. Through their conquests (as well as their migrations), they embraced different elements of native cultures, but they also influenced others enough to become the dominant culture in both Italy or the Iberian Peninsula. And since they were so close to both the Romans and the Byzantines, they can rightfully be seen as the successors of Rome in important respects. Thanks to the Goths, Roman law remained in practice long after the city of Rome had fallen under Odoacer, and the transition between Roman and post-Roman Europe was made somewhat easier with Gothic kings at the peak of their power.

One particular innovation that the Goths provided changed the entire course of warfare. While they started off as a completely infantry-based army, they were the first military force to use horses in combat. Even as far back as the Battle of Adrianople, the Gothic chieftain Fritigern would command a cavalry. Athaulf was the first ruler to openly and extensively implement horseback war tactics. Some scholars see this moment as the de facto transition between antiquity warfare and early medieval warfare.

Goths of both Eastern and Western varieties were also responsible for more than a few historic events that have since become legendary. It was the Goths who first sacked Rome in 410, and it was a series of Gothic kings who would decide on which emperor should sit on the Roman throne. It was a Gothic king that gave Attila the Hun his first major defeat, and it was another Gothic king that would unite Spain for the first time in history and declare himself independent of the waning Roman Empire. Yet another Gothic king was the one who would kill the man who destroyed the Western Roman Empire and claim the territory for himself, further expanding his kingdom and effectively ruling all of the Goths and nearly all of the Iberian and Italian Mediterranean coast. It was a Gothic priest who invented a whole new alphabet to translate the Bible into Gothic, giving us an insight into old Germanic languages of the time, and it was a Gothic queen that maintained the stability of Italy even after the death of her far more capable father. And it's the two Gothic dynasties that are responsible for shaping much of European political, ecclesiastical, and social life with their blend of Roman and Gothic customs.

History of the late 19th and early 20th centuries has not been kind to the Goths. Their association with the National Socialist German Workers' Party of Germany (the Nazis) had left a bad taste in the mouth of many historians, and sadly, terms such as "Gothic" and "Arian" can make everyday people cringe even today because of what connotations they might have. But historically speaking, the Goths of the East and the West have contributed far more, and in a far more flattering manner, to our collective memory than anything the Nazi regime did. As such, we have to approach the Gothic history scientifically but not without inquisitive curiosity, for people like the Goths, with their fascinating past, tumultuous kingdoms and fierce, legendary kings, can only leave you wanting to know a lot more.

Here's another book by Captivating History you might be interested in

Bibliography and References

Brennan, P. (1984): Diocletian and the Goths, In *Phoenix* Vol. 38, No. 2 (pp. 142-146) Toronto, CA: Classical Association of Canada

Burrell, E. (2004): A Re-Examination of Why Stilicho Abandoned His Pursuit of Alaric in 397, In *Historia: Zeitschrift für Alte Geschichte* Vol. 53, No. 2, (pp. 251-256). Stuttgart, Germany: Franz Steiner Verlag

Burns, T. S. (1982): Theories and Facts: The Early Gothic Migrations, In *History in Africa* Vol. 9 (pp. 1-20). Camden, NJ, USA: African Studies Association

Crouch, J. T. (1994): Isidore of Seville and the Evolution of Kingship in Visigothic Spain, In *Mediterranean Studies* Vol. 4, (pp. 9-26). University Park, PA, USA: Penn State University Press

Dunn, G. D. (2015): Flavius Constantius, Galla Placidia, and the Aquitanian Settlement of the Goths, In *Phoenix* Vol. 69, No. 3/4 (pp. 376-393) Toronto, CA: Classical Association of Canada

Encyclopedia Britannica (1981), Retrieved on June 18th 2019, from https://www.britannica.com

Heather, P. and Matthews, J. (2004): *The Goths in the Fourth Century*. Liverpool, UK: Liverpool University Press

Heather, P. (1995): Theoderic, King of the Goths, In *Early Medieval Europe* Vol. 4, No. 2, (pp. 146-173). Hoboken, NJ, USA: Wiley

Heather, P. (1989): Cassiodorus and the Rise of the Amals: Genealogy and the Goths under Hun Domination, In *The Journal of Roman Studies* Vol. 79, (pp. 103-128). Cambridge, UK: Society for the Promotion of Roman Studies

Livermore, H. (2006): *The Twilight of the Goths: The Rise and Fall of the Kingdom of Toledo c. 565-711*. Bristol, UK & Portland, OR, USA: Intellect Books

Moorhead, J. (1978): Boethius and Romans in Ostrogothic Service, In *Historia: Zeitschrift für Alte Geschichte* Vol. 27, No. 4, (pp. 604-612). Stuttgart, Germany: Franz Steiner Verlag

Poulter, A. (2007): Invisible Goths Within and Beyond the Roman Empire, In *Bulletin of the Institute of Classical Studies* Vol. 50, No. 91, (pp. 169-182). Hoboken, NJ, USA: Wiley

Sivan, H. (1987): On Foederati, Hospitalitas, and the Settlement of the Goths in A. D. 418, In *The American Journal of Philology* Vol. 108, No. 4, (pp. 759-772). Baltimore, MD, USA: The Johns Hopkins University Press

Whitney Mathisen, R. (1984): Emigrants, Exiles, and Survivors: Aristocratic Options in Visigothic Aquitania, In *Phoenix* Vol. 38, No. 2 (pp. 159-170) Toronto, CA: Classical Association of Canada

Wikipedia (January 15, 2001), Retrieved on June 18th 2019, from https://www.wikipedia.org/

Wolfram, H. (1990): *History of the Goths*. Berkeley, Los Angeles, CA, USA & London, UK: University of California Press

Notes on Images

[i] Original image uploaded by Fred J in 2005. Retrieved from https://commons.wikimedia.org/ on July 2019 under the following license: *Creative Commons Attribution-ShareAlike 3.0 Unported.* This license lets others remix, tweak, and build upon your work even for commercial reasons, as long as they credit you and license their new creations under the identical terms.

[ii] Original image uploaded by Manuel Parada López de Corselas on 23 January 2012. Retrieved from https://commons.wikimedia.org/ on July 2019 under the following license: *Creative Commons Attribution-ShareAlike 3.0 Unported.* This license lets others remix, tweak, and build upon your work even for commercial reasons, as long as they credit you and license their new creations under the identical terms.

[iii] Original image uploaded by Jastrow on 8 November 2006. Retrieved from https://commons.wikimedia.org/ on July 2019 under the following license: *Public Domain.* This item is in the public domain, and can be used, copied, and modified without any restrictions.

[iv] Original image uploaded by Bravkov1990 on 22 July 2012. Retrieved from https://commons.wikimedia.org/ on July 2019 under the following license: *Creative Commons Attribution-ShareAlike 3.0 Unported.* This license lets others remix, tweak, and build upon your work even for commercial reasons, as long as they credit you and license their new creations under the identical terms.

[v] Original image uploaded by Vortimer on 27 December 2007. Retrieved from https://commons.wikimedia.org/ on July 2019 under the following license: *Creative Commons Attribution-ShareAlike 3.0 Unported.* This license lets others remix, tweak, and build upon your work even for commercial reasons, as long as they credit you and license their new creations under the identical terms.

[vi] Original image uploaded by Hartmann Schedel on 21 July 2008. Retrieved from https://commons.wikimedia.org/ on July 2019 under the following license: *Public Domain*. This item is in the public domain, and can be used, copied, and modified without any restrictions.

[vii] Original image uploaded by Zaqarbal on 21 April 2006. Retrieved from https://commons.wikimedia.org/ on July 2019 under the following license: *Creative Commons Attribution-ShareAlike 3.0 Unported*. This license lets others remix, tweak, and build upon your work even for commercial reasons, as long as they credit you and license their new creations under the identical terms.

[viii] Original image uploaded by Zmiley on 10 October 2009. Retrieved from https://commons.wikimedia.org/ on July 2019 under the following license: *Public Domain*. This item is in the public domain, and can be used, copied, and modified without any restrictions.

[ix] Original image uploaded by Mabonillog on 13 September 2008. Retrieved from https://commons.wikimedia.org/ on July 2019 under the following license: *Creative Commons Attribution-ShareAlike 3.0 Unported*. This license lets others remix, tweak, and build upon your work even for commercial reasons, as long as they credit you and license their new creations under the identical terms.

[x] Original image uploaded by Kaidari on 26 March 2012. Retrieved from https://commons.wikimedia.org/ on July 2019 under the following license: *Creative Commons Attribution-ShareAlike 3.0 Unported*. This license lets others remix, tweak, and build upon your work even for commercial reasons, as long as they credit you and license their new creations under the identical terms.

[xi] Original image uploaded by Kaidari on 26 March 2012. Retrieved from https://commons.wikimedia.org/ on July 2019 under the following license: *Creative Commons Attribution-ShareAlike 3.0 Unported*. This license lets others remix, tweak, and build upon your work even for commercial reasons, as long as they credit you and license their new creations under the identical terms.

[xii] Original image uploaded by Hedning on 19 June 2011. Retrieved from https://commons.wikimedia.org/ on July 2019 under the following license: *Public Domain*. This item is in the public domain, and can be used, copied, and modified without any restrictions.

[xiii] Original image uploaded by Asta on 22 April 2006. Retrieved from https://commons.wikimedia.org/ on July 2019 under the following license: *Public Domain*. This item is in the public domain, and can be used, copied, and modified without any restrictions.

www.ingramcontent.com/pod-product-compliance
Lightning Source LLC
LaVergne TN
LVHW090038080526
838202LV00046B/3860